Wishing you
365 Days of Self Compassion
52 Weeks of Resiliency
12 Months of Healthy Boundaries

Rosa Linda Cruz Counseling & Wellness Services, LLC
Copyright 2024
ISBN: 9798884892200

All rights reserved. No part of this publication may be reproduced, stored in retrieval system or transmitted in any form, or by any means, electronic, mechanical, recorded, photocopies, or otherwise, without the prior written permission of the copyright owner, except by a reviewer who may quote brief passages in a review. The scanning, uploading, and distribution of this book via the internet or via any other means without the permission of the author is illegal and punishable by law. Please purchase on authorized electronic editions and do not participate in or encourage piracy of copy written materials.

1st Edition: March 18, 2024

The author of this book does not dispense medical advice or prescribe the use of any technique as a form of treatment for physical, emotional, or medical problems without the advice of a physician, either directly or indirectly. The intent of the author is to offer information of a general nature to assist in the journey of well being.

My Anxious Mind, Heart & Body

10 Simple Strategies a Guide to Manage Anxiety

by
Rosa Linda Cruz
LPC-S, Author & Consultant

A special thank you to my grandchildren, students and community members who continually ask for fun, engaging and interactive workbooks. My grandchildren are a source of energy and remind me to be present & live a life filled with joy, awe and wonder. My students and community members inspire me to be a life learner and to continually share mental health strategies within our communities. Your support and encouragement are sincerely appreciated and hope that you will find this resource helpful in your life journey.

Dedicated
to my Grandchildren, Students & Community Members

SUD Subjective Units of Distress

Let us begin today and assess how we have been feeling the last 2 weeks. Let's rate our stress level. I always like to give everyone a few options so choose one from the following:

Circle Stress level within the last 2 weeks:

1 bit of stress	5 some stress	10 extremely stressful
		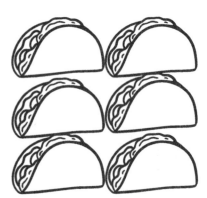

SUD Subjective Units of Distress

Let us begin today and assess how we have been feeling the last 2 weeks. Let's rate our stress level. I always like to give everyone a few options so choose one from the following:

Circle Stress level within the last 2 weeks:

1 bit of stress			5 some stress			10 extremely stressful

Window of Tolerance

It's important to know that we are hard wired to survive our world from the onset we are conceived in the womb. Our amygdala is our alarm system that detects danger and our bodies will automatically go into fight, flight, or freeze mode. This creates mental, emotional and physical changes in our nervous system. Our bodies are reacting to new situations and it helps us to stay alert, energetic and motivated. However, if we have had past traumatic events in our life this will activate our alarm system into thinking the present situation is a past event based on sensory output. We want to be in the Window of Tolerance. Please note the following descriptors.

WINDOW of TOLERANCE
Grounded Flexible Open Curious Present Safe Capable Mindful Engaged
Connected Self soothing Able to self regulate Emotionally flexible Self awareness
Emotionally regulated Connection with others Optimal problem solving Alert
Engaging Accessing emotion and reasoning Sense of safety Learn Listen

HYPERAROUSAL
Anxiety Anger Aggression Rage Fight Flight Hypervigilance Panic
Chaotic Overwhelmed Hyperactivity Intrusive imagery Rapid Breathing
Physical tension Increased heart rate Emotional distress Can't think clearly
Unproductive problem solving Want to escape Thoughts racing Out of control

HYPOAROUSAL
Passive Shutdown Numb Freeze Fatigue Shame Exhaustion Disconnection
Zoned out Unfocused Checked out Lethargic Tired Sleepy Unmotivated
Slow moving Depression Disengagement of self & others Absence of sensation
Disconnection with emotions and body Difficulty tracking conversation Collapse
Memory loss Decreased heart rate Shutting down Helpless Too scared to move

Window of Tolerance

WINDOW of TOLERANCE

Our brain is like a house with many different rooms. Each room is in charge of different things. We have access to all parts of our brain when we are in the window of tolerance. We are able to determine what is happening in our environment based on responsive thoughts and the ability to recognize that this is a false alarm. Our cognitive level is ON-LINE.

OPTIMAL ZONE   ENGAGED   COMFORTABLE

HYPERAROUSAL

Our brain which represents a house now has some closed doors and some open doors. The open doors are accessing emotions which create ripple effects of body sensations and puts us on alarm mode which may be false. The closed doors represent that our cognitive level is OFF-LINE.

EXCESSIVE ACTIVATION   MOBILIZED   OVERLOADED

HYPOAROUSAL

Our brain which represents a house has now closed all doors. It is a total shutdown and there is NO ACCESS.

AUTOPILOT   DEMOBILIZED   SHUTDOWN

Getting Started

Learning how to apply strategies in our daily life allows us space to be present and assess our situations. I gently encourage us to select one tool from the following and start to practice, apply and implement in our daily routine. The same way we brush our teeth, bathe, and put deodorant on a daily basis, is the same way we need to learn to incorporate these wonderful coping skills. This will help our mind, heart and body to connect and recognize what we are trying to do on those challenging days.

Starting our foundation is key. The most fundamental steps are to monitor our sleep, hydration, nourishment and connection.

Sleep is essential for all human beings. Lack of sleep impairs our brain's functioning including our ability to remember, regulate emotion and attention, the speed we process information and the ability to have insight.

Hydration allows us to replenish our fluid intake. Lack of it creates low energy levels, fatigue and strength. Dehydration also impacts moodiness. confusion and tension.

Eat well balanced meals that include fruits, vegetables, healthy carbohydrates and lean proteins. Try avoiding processed foods, sugary junk food and unhealthy snacks.

Connection is essential for all us. Taking time to maintain healthy relationships can lead to better life and improved well being. It creates a sense of belonging, being cared for, valued and supported.

Getting Started

Our foundation and techniques that we incorporate should be a part of our daily life. As the weeks progress, add more tools so we can have an abundance of mental health strategies to choose from.

Our brain is an amazing organ. It has the ability to rewire and create new thoughts and patterns of behavior. It takes practice. We need to give ourselves the patience, kindness and love that we deserve to learn how to respond in a healthier way.

There are some essential steps to this: Pause, Breathe, Notice-Observe-Non-Judgmental, Neutral Space, Event, Thoughts, Feelings, Body Sensations & Behaviors.

When in the midst of overwhelming feelings and body sensations, this is the first thing we notice. It is imperative that we literally PAUSE. Our first step PAUSE gives us the time and space to transition into our next step.

The second step is BREATHE. We can choose to apply a breathing technique, ground ourselves using our senses, put cold water on our face, drink a warm cup of tea, sit in nature, walk away from the environment, or stretch. There are many options available to us. Please note we need to practice our techniques daily so when we are immersed in a moment of large waves of emotions and pounding of somatic sensations, our mind, heart and body will respond more effectively when in the middle of the stormy weather.

Getting Started

The third step is NOTICE, OBSERVE, & be NON-JUDGMENTAL. When we take time to NOTICE that these feelings are visiting, it allows us to OBSERVE if they are a false alarm or a real alarm. Being NON-JUDGMENTAL allows our mind, heart and body to shift into the next step.

Please note that this transition takes time. Practice self compassion and take time to be kind, patient and love ourselves in this moment. Be Non-Judgmental.

The fourth step is NEUTRAL SPACE. By this time our nervous system should be in a calmer state. The shifting of gears from dysregulated emotions and dysregulated body sensations should be more manageable. This helps us to access our cognitive part of the brain.

What is the EVENT that spiraled those thoughts? emotions? and body sensations? Describe the EVENT in a neutral way. State only the facts. Keep it bland.

Review your THOUGHTS about the EVENT. Access the evidence, facts and supported data to evaluate and assess. This helps to filter out all or nothing thinking, mind reading, personalization, overgeneralization, magnification, minimization or fortune telling.

Evaluating and creating new thoughts allows us to create new FEELINGS, new BODY SENSATIONS and new BEHAVIORS.

Getting Started

PRACTICE, APPLY & IMPLEMENT in daily routine:

SLEEP
HYDRATION
NUTRITION
CONNECTION

Limit Social Media and News

PAUSE
BREATHE
NOTICE, OBSERVE & NON-JUDGMENTAL

NEUTRAL SPACE

EVENT

THOUGHTS (facts and evidence)

FEELINGS

BODY SENSATIONS

BEHAVIORS

Examples

PAUSE
BREATHE
NOTICE, OBSERVE & NON-JUDGMENTAL

NEUTRAL SPACE

EVENT *Example*
I failed the exam.

THOUGHTS (facts and evidence) *Before and After Examples*
I'm a loser. I always fail everything. I will be grounded forever.
I pass my exams when I study daily and attend tutorials. I need to incorporate my study schedule every day.

FEELINGS *Before and After Examples*
angry, sad and defeated
optimistic, inspired and happy

BODY SENSATIONS *Before and After Examples*
tension and fast heart rate
relaxed and calm

BEHAVIORS *Before and After Examples*
throwing things around
organizing materials to study and setting a schedule

Examples

PAUSE
BREATHE
NOTICE, OBSERVE & NON-JUDGMENTAL

NEUTRAL SPACE

EVENT *Example*
I started a new job.

THOUGHTS (facts and evidence) *Before and After Examples*
I don't have friends. I don't know anything. I will never get this.
It takes time to form friendships, learn new things and create a new routine.

FEELINGS *Before and After Examples*
overwhelmed, frustrated and worried
confident, trusting and courageous

BODY SENSATIONS *Before and After Examples*
stomach knots and on edge
strong and clear headed

BEHAVIORS *Before and After Examples*
sitting around and moping
reaching out to connect, studying extra to learn regulations and recognizing productive times that are effective

CHAIR YOGA

Let's get started with this stretching exercise.

Get into a comfortable seated position.
We may choose to close our eyes or look downward.
Take a deep breath in and take a deep breath out. (Repeat 4x)

Gently move our head to the right side and hold for a few seconds.
Center our head.
Gently move our head to the left side and hold for a few seconds. (Repeat 4x)
Take a deep breath in and take a deep breath out.

Gently roll our shoulders back on a count of of eight.
Gently roll our shoulders forward on a count of eight.
Take a deep breath in and take a deep breath out.

Gently wiggle our fingers and stretch our arms outward as if reaching for something.
Gently bring our arms back in and wiggle our fingers. (Repeat 4x)
Take a deep breath in and take a deep breath out.

Gently rotate our wrists outward on a count of eight.
Gently rotate our wrists inward on a count of eight.
Take a deep breath in and take a deep breath out.

Gently turn our torso to the right and hold for a few seconds.
Center our torso.
Gently turn our torso to the left and hold for a few seconds. (Repeat 4x)
Take a deep breath in and take a deep breath out.

Raise both legs and point toes outward and hold for a few seconds.
Keep both legs up and point toes inward and hold for a few seconds. (Repeat 4x)
Take a deep breath in and take a deep breath out. (Repeat 4x)

CHAIR YOGA

There are many benefits to practicing chair yoga on a daily basis.

Decreases stress
Increases circulation
Builds strength
Maintains and improves mental clarity
Feelings of well being
Improves coordination
Increases flexibility
Effective
Accessible
Allows for refocus and concentration

Reflection:

When is a good time to practice, apply and implement chair yoga in your daily routine?

What kind of feelings do you get after this exercise?

Where do you feel them in your body?

What are your thoughts after this exercise?

How will this help you in your daily life?

BREATHE

Let's get started with a simple breathing exercise.

Get comfortable in a seated position. We may choose to close our eyes or look downward.
Sit still for just a few minutes.
Place one hand on our chest and the other hand on our tummy.
Place our feet to the ground.
Listen to our breath.
Focus on the inhale and exhale.
Inhale deeply and hold for a few seconds.
Exhale deeply.
Repeat 8x

Practice kindness, patience and love for ourselves.
Just notice, observe and be non-judgmental.

Keep in mind that when we practice our breathing it is important we take a deep breath in, hold for a few seconds and extend our breath out longer.

"Our breath nourishes our body, bathes our tissues, and brings in energy."
by Dr. Bessel Van Der Kolk, The Body Keeps the Score

BREATHE

There are many benefits to using breathing techniques on a daily basis.

Regulates
Recovers
Restores
Lowers stress
Lowers heart rate and blood pressure
Reduces tension
Relaxes
Reduces level of stress hormones in the body
Increases feelings of calm and wellbeing
Increases energy

Reflection:

When is a good time to practice, apply and implement breathing techniques in your daily routine?

What kind of feelings do you get after this exercise?

Where do you feel it in your body?

What are your thoughts after this exercise?

How will this help you in your daily life?

BREATHE

Here are some additional fun bonus breathing techniques for all ages.

Shoulder Breath Roll
take a deep breath in while pulling shoulders up towards the ears
then
take a deep breath out while dropping the shoulders back
repeat 8x

Taco Breath
curl the edges of your tongue together like a taco
take a deep breath in through the taco
hold the breath for a few seconds
then gently breathe out through the nose
repeat 8x

Bumble Bee Breath
breathe in deeply and slowly keeping mouth closed
make a humming noise while breathing out
repeat 8x

BREATHE

Here are some additional fun bonus breathing techniques for all ages.

Volcano Breath
pretend hands and arms are like lava flowing from a volcano
start with hands in front of the heart with palms touching
keeping hands together reach straight up and breathe in
separate hands and move arms down to the side of your body and breathe out
repeat 8x

Dragon Breath
interlace fingers under the chin
breathe in and raise elbows as high as possible
breathe out and lower elbows back down
repeat 8x

Hot Air Balloon Breath
cup hands around the mouth and breathe in deeply
and
while breathing out expand hands outward as if blowing up a great hot air balloon
repeat 8x

RANDOM ACTS OF KINDNESS

Here are a few examples of random acts of kindness to get you started.

Encourage someone
Write a thank you note
Volunteer
Take time to listen to a friend
Write a positive note on a post it and place it on someone's desk
Be grateful
Speak kindly
Give a genuine compliment
Hold a foodbank drive
Surprise someone with a treat
Do a chore without being asked
Smile at someone new
Send a gratitude email

RANDOM ACTS OF KINDNESS

There are many benefits to implementing random acts of kindness on a daily basis.

Generates endorphins creates good feelings
Creates emotional warmth
Increases oxytocin creates positive feelings
Positive mood
Increases energy
Feelings of self worth
Optimism
Increases serotonin creates sense of well being
Calm
Increases sense of connectivity with others

Reflection:

When is a good time to practice, apply and implement random acts of kindness in your daily routine?

What kind of feelings do you get after this exercise?

Where do you feel them in your body?

What are your thoughts after this exercise?

How will this help you in your daily life?

MUSIC

I had the privilege of attending a conference where the presenter shared a research project in which a study was done on plants.

The first group of plants that received sunshine and water thrived and flourished.

The second group of plants that did not receive sunshine and water consistently withered away.

The last group of plants that did not receive sunshine and water consistently but had music in the background managed to thrive and flourish much better than the second group.

It made me start thinking of how often do I incorporate music in my day. What's the first thing I turn on while I am getting ready for the day. The news? and what am I hearing? It does not mean by any account that I should be dismissive of what is happening in our world but what if I started the day with my favorite music.

I would gently encourage us to incorporate music in our morning routine. If possible, implement it throughout our day as background music. Playing our favorite tunes to finalize the evening has many benefits. This is also a great transition tool that can be implemented when we go from a working environment to our home environment. We may even want to add a little singing and dancing.

MUSIC

There are many benefits in listening to music on a daily basis.

Increases energy
Happiness
Improves cognitive performance
Enhances movement
Lowers stress
Improves sleep
Elevates mood
Strengthens learning and memory
Reduces anxiety
Boosts your concentration and focus

Reflection:

When is a good time to practice, apply and implement music in your daily routine?

What kind of feelings do you get after this exercise?

Where do you feel them in your body?

What are your thoughts after this exercise?

How will this help you in your daily life?

Journaling

Research still supports journaling as a way to process thoughts and feelings on daily events, past memories, challenges and daily moments of gratefulness. This can consist of writing, making lists, drawing, sketching or coloring.

Ideas to implement journaling:
Start with our feelings and emotions
Describe the body sensations
Explain the thoughts creating the feelings and emotions
Describe the event in simplest format that is creating those thoughts

Review facts, evidence and data that support thoughts
Create new perspectives and new insights
List different approaches to what is happening
List resources, skills and techniques
Shifting gears can create new feelings and new behaviors
Make a list of the worse case scenarios, best case scenarios and balance responses

Keep it simple
Be creative
Write a poem about it
Create a comic strip on the events
Make a song
Color your feelings
Create a new narrative

Journaling

There are many benefits to journaling on a daily basis.

Focuses on emotional experience and thoughts
Focuses on positive aspects of life
Reduces anxiety
Allows time to review thoughts
Regulates emotions
Encourages awareness
Releases and processes emotions
Improves awareness and perceptions
Helps to track progress and growth
Improves communication skills

Reflection:

When is a good time to practice, apply and implement journaling in your daily routine?

Where kind of feelings do you get after this exercise?

Where you feel them in your body?

What are your thoughts after this exercise?

How will this help you in your daily life?

Sunshine Corner

Grounding ourselves means taking a moment to pause, place feet on the ground and be present. Take a moment to incorporate our senses which include sight, smell, hear, taste and touch. I gently encourage us to take time to surround ourselves with items that bring calm, inner joy and incorporate visual, auditory, olfactory, gustatory and tactile sensations to our environment.

In addition, we may ground ourselves the following ways:
Walk barefoot in the sand, grass or dirt
Press bare hands into the grass or earth
Float in a body of water
Garden with our bare hands in soil
Dig holes in the beach sand
Sit on an area where we are able to place our bare feet flat on the earth

Surround ourselves with the following:
Favorite photos of loved ones
Accessible music playing in the background
Use a diffuser with favorite oils
Have a handful of mints nearby
Place a favorite blanket or sweater nearby

Sunshine Corner

There are many benefits to applying grounding on a daily basis.

Elevates mood
Increases energy level
Improves sleep quality
Reduces stress
Improves physical function
Decreases fatigue and tiredness
Improves cortisol rhythm the stress level is reduced
Encourages calmness
Stronger immune system functioning
Feels centered, strong and solid

Reflection:

When is a good time to practice, apply and implement grounding in your daily routine?

Where kind of feelings do you get after this exercise?

Where you feel them in your body?

What are your thoughts after this exercise?

How will this help you in your daily life?

Laughter Yoga

Dr. Madan Kataria is the creator of laughter exercises. During his research, he discovered there was a field of pioneers who initially studied the psychological and physiological affects of incorporating laughter in our daily life. His laugher yoga is now in over 72 countries. The benefits of laughter exercises are incorporated by many educational, professional and medical organizations.

Our mind, heart and body begin to immediately register new changes when laughter is introduced. Those changes include lowering of the cortisol stress levels, an increase in endorphins the good feeling hormones, more oxygen, increased circulation and a surge of dopamine which activates pleasure in our system. "The physical, emotional, mental and social connection between laughter allows bursts of energy, a better outlook on life, alleviates stress and so much more."

Gentle ways of incorporating inner joy is surrounding ourselves with loved ones, having game nights with our friends, watching comedy movies, attending musical concerts, enrolling in pottery or art classes, taking dance classes, creating new hobbies or interests, journaling daily on wins, accomplishments, acts of kindness and grateful moments, engaging in volunteer work, and participating in exercise classes.

"Our bodies do not know the difference between genuine and fake laughter."
Ha Ha Ha Ha Ha Ha Ha Ha Ha Ha Ha Ha Ha Ha Ha Ha Ha Ha Ha Ha
He He He He He He He He He He He He He He He He He He He He
Ho Ho Ho Ho Ho Ho Ho Ho Ho Ho Ho Ho Ho Ho Ho Ho Ho Ho Ho Ho

Laughter Yoga

There are many benefits to implementing laughter exercises on a daily basis.

Improves mood
Alleviates stress
Boosts immune system
Lowers stress hormone
Relaxes the body
Enhances resilience
Gives more energy
Promotes better sleep
Increases endorphins the happy feeling
Adds joy to our life

Reflection:

When is a good time to practice, apply and implement laughter exercises in your daily routine?

Where kind of feelings do you get after this exercise?

Where you feel them in your body?

What are your thoughts after this exercise?

How will this help you in your daily life?

Progressive Relaxation

This exercise is a great way to get our mind and body in sync. Sometime we experience moments when we may be physically and mentally exhausted. Yet, when we go to bed our body is literally exhausted yet our brain is still running a 100 miles per hour. This body scan allows us to acknowledge our stressors and release them away.

Try this progressive relaxation exercise. We will tense parts of our body muscles and relax them. Then tense the whole body. We may tense and relax on increments of 7 to 12 seconds.

Tense toes
Relax toes
Tense calves
Relax calves
Tense thighs
Relax thighs
Tense tiny hiny
Relax tiny hiny
Tense back and shoulders
Relax back and shoulders
Tense arms and hands
Relax arms and hands
Tense face
Relax face
Tense whole body
Relax whole body
(Repeat 8x)

Progressive Relaxation

There are many benefits to practicing progressive relaxation on a daily basis.

Decreases anxiety and stress
Improves ability to fall and stay asleep
Relieves tension
Enhances awareness and connection
Creates physiological changes
Lowers cortisol levels stress hormone
Decreases flight or fight mode
Improves insight
Eases tense muscles
Controls anxiety response

Reflection:

When is a good time to practice, apply and implement progressive relaxation in your daily routine?

Where kind of feelings do you get after this exercise?

Where you feel them in your body?

What are your thoughts after this exercise?

How will this help you in your daily life?

Bonus Strategy

Happy Place
Name a place that is real or imaginary that gives you calm and happy feelings.
Describe your happy place using your senses.
Describe or draw everything you see, hear, smell, taste and/or touch.

Please note it's okay if you don't use all of your senses. This is your happy place and it can be described or drawn anyway you like.

What kind of feelings do you get when you imagine yourself in this happy place?

Where in your body do you get those feelings?

What do you believe about yourself when you are in your happy place?
I am _____
I am _____
I am _____

Let's Practice:
When you are ready, close your eyes, take a deep breath in, hold, breathe out and imagine you are in your happy place.
Notice all the amazing images, scents, sounds, tastes and textures.
Notice the feelings and where they reside in your body.
Notice what you believe about yourself. I am_____
Take your time immersing yourself in this wonderful place you have created.
When you have finished this exercise, take a deep breath in, hold, breathe out and gently open your eyes.

Bonus Strategy
describe or draw your happy place here

Reflection:

What kind of feelings do you get after this exercise?

Where do you feel them in your body?

What are your thoughts after this exercise?

How will this help you in your daily life?

Gentle Reminders

Additional Strategies to incorporate in your daily routine

Exercise
Yoga
Paint
Garden
Music
Meditation
Dance
Color
Sing
Walk
Nature
Crochet
Surf
Read
Sketch
Play
Bubbles
Hobby
Prayer
Volunteer
Laugh
Journaling
Grounding
Earthing
Breathing techniques
Talk to a trusted adult

Gentle Reminders

Practice, Apply and Implement on a daily basis - make it part of your routine

---

Sleep, Hydrate, Nourish & Connect

Limit Social Media & News

Pause

Breathe (grounding, walking, drinking warm tea, splashing cold water on face, listen to music, or choose any technique that will help you calm and soothe your nervous system. Practice kindness and patience to yourself.)

Notice, Observe and be Non-Judgmental (feelings are temporary visitors)

Neutral Space (allows you to transition to the cognitive level-evaluate, analyze, assess and make a new plan of action, gain new insights and perspectives)

EVENT (keep it simple and neutral)

THOUGHTS (review the facts and evidence to dispute or counter the original thoughts)

FEELINGS (new thoughts create new feelings)

BODY SENSATIONS (new feelings create new body sensations)

BEHAVIORS (new body sensations create new behaviors)

What I learned today

What I learned today

My favorite techniques

My favorite techniques

Other tools I can use

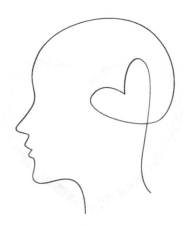

Other tools I can use

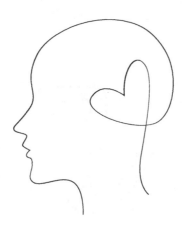

I can talk to_____
when I am out of my window of tolerance

I can talk to_____
when I am out of my window of tolerance

Learning techniques are important because

Learning techniques are important because

Additional Worksheet

Let us begin today and assess how we have been feeling the last 2 weeks. Let's rate our stress level. I always like to give everyone a few options so choose one from the following:

Circle Stress level within the last 2 weeks:

1 bit of stress   5 some stress   10 extremely stressful

Additional Worksheet

PRACTICE, APPLY & IMPLEMENT in daily routine:

PAUSE
BREATHE
NOTICE, OBSERVE & NON-JUDGMENTAL

NEUTRAL SPACE

EVENT

THOUGHTS (facts and evidence)

FEELINGS

BODY SENSATIONS

BEHAVIORS

Reflection:

What kind of feelings do you get after this exercise?

Where do you feel them in your body?

What are your thoughts after this exercise?

How will this help you in your daily life?

Additional Worksheet

Let us begin today and assess how we have been feeling the last 2 weeks. Let's rate our stress level. I always like to give everyone a few options so choose one from the following:

Circle Stress level within the last 2 weeks:

1 bit of stress   5 some stress   10 extremely stressful

Additional Worksheet

PRACTICE, APPLY & IMPLEMENT in daily routine:

PAUSE
BREATHE
NOTICE, OBSERVE & NON-JUDGMENTAL

NEUTRAL SPACE

EVENT

THOUGHTS (facts and evidence)

FEELINGS

BODY SENSATIONS

BEHAVIORS

Reflection:

What kind of feelings do you get after this exercise?

Where do you feel them in your body?

What are your thoughts after this exercise?

How will this help you in your daily life?

Additional Worksheet

Let us begin today and assess how we have been feeling the last 2 weeks. Let's rate our stress level. I always like to give everyone a few options so choose one from the following:

Circle Stress level within the last 2 weeks:

1 bit of stress   5 some stress   10 extremely stressful

  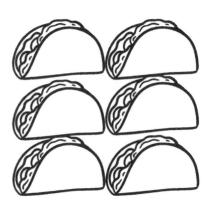

Additional Worksheet

PRACTICE, APPLY & IMPLEMENT in daily routine:

PAUSE
BREATHE
NOTICE, OBSERVE & NON-JUDGMENTAL

NEUTRAL SPACE

EVENT

THOUGHTS (facts and evidence)

FEELINGS

BODY SENSATIONS

BEHAVIORS

Reflection:

What kind of feelings do you get after this exercise?

Where do you feel them in your body?

What are your thoughts after this exercise?

How will this help you in your daily life?

Additional Worksheet

Let us begin today and assess how we have been feeling the last 2 weeks. Let's rate our stress level. I always like to give everyone a few options so choose one from the following:

Circle Stress level within the last 2 weeks:

1 bit of stress   5 some stress   10 extremely stressful

Additional Worksheet

PRACTICE, APPLY & IMPLEMENT in daily routine:

PAUSE
BREATHE
NOTICE, OBSERVE & NON-JUDGMENTAL

NEUTRAL SPACE

EVENT

THOUGHTS (facts and evidence)

FEELINGS

BODY SENSATIONS

BEHAVIORS

Reflection:

What kind of feelings do you get after this exercise?

Where do you feel them in your body?

What are your thoughts after this exercise?

How will this help you in your daily life?

Additional Worksheet

Let us begin today and assess how we have been feeling the last 2 weeks. Let's rate our stress level. I always like to give everyone a few options so choose one from the following:

Circle Stress level within the last 2 weeks:

1 bit of stress   5 some stress   10 extremely stressful

      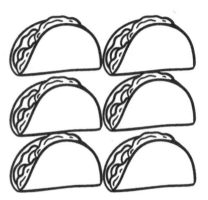

Additional Worksheet

PRACTICE, APPLY & IMPLEMENT in daily routine:

PAUSE
BREATHE
NOTICE, OBSERVE & NON-JUDGMENTAL

NEUTRAL SPACE

EVENT

THOUGHTS (facts and evidence)

FEELINGS

BODY SENSATIONS

BEHAVIORS

Reflection:

What kind of feelings do you get after this exercise?

Where do you feel them in your body?

What are your thoughts after this exercise?

How will this help you in your daily life?

Additional Worksheet

Let us begin today and assess how we have been feeling the last 2 weeks. Let's rate our stress level. I always like to give everyone a few options so choose one from the following:

Circle Stress level within the last 2 weeks:

1 bit of stress   5 some stress   10 extremely stressful

Additional Worksheet

PRACTICE, APPLY & IMPLEMENT in daily routine:

PAUSE
BREATHE
NOTICE, OBSERVE & NON-JUDGMENTAL

NEUTRAL SPACE

EVENT

THOUGHTS (facts and evidence)

FEELINGS

BODY SENSATIONS

BEHAVIORS

Reflection:

What kind of feelings do you get after this exercise?

Where do you feel them in your body?

What are your thoughts after this exercise?

How will this help you in your daily life?

NOTES:

NOTES:

NOTES:

NOTES:

Cited Resources:
https://traumaresearchfoundation.org/
https://grief.com/
https://laughteryoga.org/
https://greatergood.berkeley.edu/
https://emdrresearchfoundation.org/toolkit/butterfly-hug.pdf
https://www.mayoclinic.org/

Dr. Bessel Van Der Kolk   *The Body Keeps the Score*
Dr. Francine Shapiro   *Getting Past Your Past*
David Kessler   *Finding Meaning*
Jeannie Wycherley   *Losing My Best Friend*
Dr. Margaret Wehrenberg   *10 Best Ever Managing Techniques Anxious*
Dr. Margaret Wehrenberg   *10 Best Ever Managing Techniques Depression*
Dr. Marsha M. Linehan   *Building a Life Worth Living*
Dr. Daniel Siegel   *Now Maps   The Whole Brain Child*
Dr. Justin Coulson   *The Resilient Child   Happier Family*
Dr. Laurel Parnell   *Tapping In EMDR*

Support Resources:
Emergency Services
911 or 988
National Suicide Prevention Lifeline
1-800-273-8255
The Trevor Project
1-866-488-7386
Crisis Text Support Line
741-741

Made in the USA
Middletown, DE
04 May 2024